I'm Winning
ALL THE TIME

DONALD ROBINSON

I'm Winning All The Time

Copyright ©2015 by Donald Robinson

All rights reserved. No part of this book may be reproduced, copied, stored or transmitted in any form or by any means – graphic, electronic, or mechanical, including photocopying, recording, or information storage and retrieval systems without the prior written permission of Donald Robinson or Hope of Vision Publishing except where permitted by law.

Scripture taken from the King James Version. Copyright © 1982 by Thomas Nelson, Inc. Used by permission. All rights reserved. Holy Bible, King James Version /Amplified Version. Copyright © 1995 by Zondervan. Used by permission. All rights reserved.

HOV Publishing a division of HOV, LLC.
www.hovpub.com
hopeofvision@gmail.com

Cover Design: Hope of Vision Designs
Editor/Proofreader: Phyllis M. Bridges

Write the Author Donald Robinson at:
Email: lucyrobinson08@yahoo.com

For more information about special discounts for bulk purchases, please contact Donald Robinson or hopeofvision@gmail.com

ISBN: 978-1-942871-07-1
Library of Congress Control Number: 2015954390

10 9 8 7 6 5 4 3 2 1

Printed in the United States of America

Dedication

This book is dedicated to my precious wife, Lucille Annette Sneed - Robinson. Because of her love and faithfulness with much support, I have the freedom to boldly pursue every God given assignment. Her encouragement and support has caused me to press ahead in life when it would have been easier to just quit.... give up. Many of my dreams have become a reality because of Lucille.

I'm Winning All The Time

ACKNOWLEDGEMENTS

I would like to take this time to acknowledge some very important people who have played such a vital role in the writing and success of this book. I love my VFC family (Vision For Christ Ministries), the place to be. To all five of our children, I truly love you. I thank God for my mom, who I love and who has supported me throughout my whole life. To my parents, I strongly say thank you. To my siblings and all my relatives, I say I love you. To my sweet heart Lucille, I love you. Lastly, one Sunday morning while in church, this special lady prophesied to me about how God had spoken to her and told her to tell me that I would be writing a book and many people would support me in making it a success. Her name is Mother Stevenson. To Mother Stevenson, I truly say thanks!

Content

9	Prologue
13	CHAPTER 1: Experience
33	CHAPTER 2: Gathering Enough Biblical Knowledge
39	CHAPTER 3: Renewing The Mind
45	CHAPTER 4: The Law of A Negative Environment
55	CHAPTER 5: The Law of A Positive Environment
63	CHAPTER 6: Learning to Manage One's Soul
73	CHAPTER 7: A New Meaning
83	CHAPTER 8: Biblical Belief
87	CHAPTER 9: Biblical Faith
95	CHAPTER 10: Release Your Faith
109	CHAPTER 11: Patience
115	About The Author

I'm Winning All The Time

Prologue

Start Date: November 29, 2008
Time: 5:08pm
Day: Saturday, my first book

Stop, listen and read! I can do all things through Christ who strengthens me! Because Christ believes in me, all things are possible if I can choose to believe what He believes about me. Though my thought sounds one way, my heart (spirit) tells me another thing.... Believe! What Christ says about me is, "I'm a winner." I win with Him and through Him. To win, I must concentrate primarily on the truth (God's word) and not only the facts (my situations), because the truth can change the facts. This makes this subject a personal one, being that I realize and recognize that God has done great and marvelous things for me. For if it had not been for my God, the Strong Tower, on my side, I do not know where I would be today.

So, I write this book with great passion. This passion and inspiration is derived from one Saturday morning while lying in my bed beside my beautiful wife, Lucille, talking to her about the many different challenges we were experiencing at that moment. As God used her to say, "Though we are being challenged in many areas, yet we are still winning. We are winners. We are more than conquerors through Christ. We always win, no matter what." We win because He says so!

Immediately, I heard God's voice as clear as a sunny day. His voice was providing me with the subject of this book, while instructing me to write this book. As days passed, I began to write this book. It was on a Saturday evening, November 29, 2008, at approximately 5:08 PM.

As you read this book, my goal is to inspire, motivate and encourage each reader. This inspiring book is for all who will read it, learn from it and skillfully and properly apply it's principals.

I'm Winning All The Time

Chapter 1:

Experience

While attending Blanche Ely High School from 1985 -1986, I did not know what to do as my graduation day was approaching. My awesome basketball season was about to end, I had just three months left before graduation and I had yet to decide where I wanted to go from there. Growing up, I did not notice, nor have any great role models around to follow, leaving it very tough for me to decide my next move in life. I always wanted something in life, but I did not know how to go about accomplishing it. I did not see great men around whom I could say I would like to be like. One may say your dad... he's your great role model. Yes... that's true, but I did not get to know my dad until I was 17 years old and getting ready to graduate from High School. Our relationship had not developed at that time. So, knowing what to do was extremely difficult for me. It was very challenging. Notice, I did not say impossible. My mom was great. She was always around and dependable, as she is today. So, in the fall of 1986, after graduating from High School, I enrolled in Broward Community College located in Coconut Creek, Florida. At that time, I was still unsure as to what I wanted to do. I knew I desired to be successful, rich and a great man of God, but I just did not know how to accomplish being successful and rich. My problem was I did not know how to turn my desire into a reality; this was my biggest struggle. I remember asking myself over and over again, how is this going to work within a quick time when I didn't know or understand the particulars. See, I wanted success very quickly. After a year in college, as I pondered how I needed to be further along in life, I drifted away and into selling drugs; crack cocaine to be precise. This behavior began due to me being unsure as to what I wanted to do in life, getting unfocused and watching my friend with loads of cash every day; more than I had ever seen before. I asked him where did he get that amount of cash from. He said, "Selling drugs." I never became a user, I was only a dealer. Thoughts were entering my mind saying, "This is your way to become successful and rich." As loads of cash came in, I became more and more convinced that this was my way to get whatever I'd desired for years. By this time, I was only 18 years old. Remember, my mom did not raise me and my siblings this way. We were never exposed to such a lifestyle. There was never any liquor nor narcotics ever around us. She taught us respect, to love ourselves, each other, others and God. She also taught us to work hard in life to earn whatever we wanted, as you can be and have what you believe and work hard for; that is the right way of course. I was living a lifestyle contrary to how mom raised us. As I was living this lifestyle, I started smoking pot daily, though I was stilled enrolled in college. I thought trying out for college basketball would help me redirect my focus and reprogram my direction. I attend basketball practice regularly, I earned a college basketball scholarship. I continued playing basketball while attending school for nearly one year. The load became very stressful, I was arrested shortly after. Later, I was sentenced to serve 4 ½ years in the Florida State Prison.

Everything quickly changed. Because this was my first offense, I was sent to Florida's "Boot Camp" for 90 to 120 days. This boot camp was designed to give youth and first time offenders an opportunity to rearrange their lives for the better, to give all youth offenders a new perspective on life. While there, I had much time to think about how I drifted away. As I thought things through wisely, I learned that I could start over. I could re-write the chapters of my life. My life was not over because I chose a wrong decision. I used this experience to learn how to become successful and rich God's way. After completing the boot camp program successfully, I was released. I knew there would be different types of challenges than those I faced before being an ex-con.

Shortly after my release, I landed a warehouse job. I was there for about 2 years. Then, I got another job. This was a driver's job. Again, I knew I was entitled to having the best, but I just did not know how to earn it the right way. This driver's job lasted for 1 ½ years. So, I went from job to job feeling bad about my life and knowing that I could have more. So, I re-enrolled in Broward Community College. By this time, I was 20 years old. This time, my mind was more committed, determined and focus. I was not going to let nothing get in my way as before. I was attending college full-time. While there, I earned an academic scholarship. Life was looking bright for me. This lasted for about 1½ years. I finally graduated from Broward Community College with an Associate Degree in Prelaw. I immediately transferred my education to Florida Atlantic University located in Boca Raton, Florida. I enrolled to earn a Bachelor Degree of Arts, with a major in Political Science. By this time, I thought I wanted to be a lawyer, a corporate attorney. While attending Florida Atlantic University part-time and working, I was doing well for the years enrolled. During this time, I heard God's voice speak to me saying, "You will not pass the necessary exams to earn this degree if you do not serve me with your whole heart. This helped me to understand that God was getting me ready to win. You must get ready to win. Winning takes preparation. Nothing will be impossible unto you with me as the center of your life." I said wow, God! I knew exactly what God was saying. Not long after hearing from God, I began to seek God for a wife. I was very clear as to what I was looking for in a wife. Yes, you must be clear and specific with God, as you should be with anyone else, right? Therefore, of the friend girls I had, I quickly released everyone, except the one who I was waiting for. I completely left every old lifestyle behind, not ever looking back in terms of selling drugs, smoking pot and having different friend girls. When she finally came to me, we dated for one year. During this time, we talked about what was most important in our lives. We discussed what we wanted in life. There were many different questions we asked each other before we said I do. We did not get any spiritual counseling before we got married, but later in the marriage we did. Finally, we got married as we both surrendered our lives totally to God. I left every old lifestyle I had behind. We both were extremely hungry and thirsty for God. Then God spoke to me and told me to tell my newlywed wife, "God said for me to stop working and attend school full-time." She said to me, "You have bumped your head. You must be crazy. How could we make it? Go seek God again for He could not have said that." I began to pray to God to reveal unto her what He revealed unto me. Not many days later, He did just that. So, I stopped working to attend school full-time for the duration. As we touched and agreed, every bill we had was met, and we had more money available this way than we had when both of us were working. We were quickly learning serving God and living by faith is good! I did receive both financial aid (grant funds) and student loans. In April of 1999, I earned my second degree, a Bachelor of Arts Degree, with a major in Political Science from Florida Atlantic University. From there, I attempted to apply to several law schools for admission. The last Law school was Emory University School Of law, located in Atlanta, Georgia. My wife and I decided to visit the law school for the admission's process. The visitation was great. Everything looked promising. When we reached home expecting to relocate, God speaks to me about ministry. Later, I learned that was my call into ministry. At that time, being an attorney was not what God wanted for me. This caused me to go into a prayer time to seek God like never before to find out what God would like for me to do. Remember, I thought at the time I was to be an attorney; that was what I wanted to be. So, we ended up not relocating to Atlanta. We stayed in Florida where I became a youth Pastor for five years. I am currently a Senior Pastor of a thriving ministry. I strongly believe Pastoring was what God wanted me to do.

As time continued, the year of 2008 became the most challenging year ever in our marriage. When I heard and learned that the year of 2007 was the year of "Completion," while 2008 was the year of a "New Beginning", I automatically thought that it was all over for our struggles and lack. I thought to myself and aloud, "Out with the old problems and in with the overflow of God's blessings and promises." Remember, it was the year of completion and the year of a new beginning. I did not know that God's blessings and promises are not all given automatically. So, can you see how I could have thought this way? Do you think this way?

In other words, I thought of it in just one way, in terms of I'm starting over in a way with God that would automatically cause me to receive God's divine blessings, experience God's breakthrough like never before; and experience God more than enough to cause overflow in every area of my life. In fact, is this not the purpose for Jesus' coming? Not to say this is His only reason for coming to Earth, but scriptures make it clear that He wants His children to have an abundant life. Live abundantly. Enjoy life abundantly. Give abundantly and receive abundantly. Right! Again, I had to discover that God's blessings are not given and received automatically.

For example, in the book of John 10:10b

(AMP) it reads Jesus' purpose being "I come that they may have and enjoy life, and have it in abundance (to the full, till it overflows)." Instead, however, the opposite was happening. Have you ever thought that things are supposed to just automatically happen for you because of what you have read and/or heard preached? It seemed as though I was losing everything, my mind, marriage, home, automobile, business (child-care), ministry and even losing contact with God. It was as though He was nowhere to be found and completely out of my reach. I even began to think that my prayers were not being heard nor answered because I was not seeing and experiencing a difference in our situations fast enough.

Have situations ever appeared to be this way to you? Have you felt as though you were actually alone because you were not seeing and experiencing God's best fast enough after you prayed and heard the word of God, even the word of faith preached?

I viewed these challenges, barriers and even obstacles totally opposite of Jesus' purpose for dwelling on Earth. Walls were so high in our lives that we just could not see our way. The high walls blocked our view for a better life. Through every moment and movement it seemed as though our lives were falling down. Nothing seemed to be working in our favor. The facts of life had really taken ahold of us. We were experiencing financial difficulties like never before, our marriage was strongly being negatively challenged as a direct result and life just did not seem fun and exciting anymore. The truth appeared to be unheard of because of the facts of life. At this moment, we were unaware of how to knowingly separate the difference between the facts and the truth. Although Oxford Dictionary defines the word fact(s) as: actual occurrence, reality and the truth while the bible teaches the Christian about the difference between earthly (facts) and spiritual (heavenly) principles of life. So, what we were actually going through may have been the facts, but scriptures teach that the facts can be changed by the truth. Somehow we allowed the facts to still our focus as it had stolen our joy. What we were experiencing really became our reality as it appeared to be no way out. We were being moved by our emotions.... senses instead of The Word of God.....The Word of Faith....The Word of Truth. How often does this happen in the life of the believer? What he or she may be going through at the moment really becomes his or her reality as the truth.

To me, life just did not seem enjoyable and fun anymore. Attending church did not seem exciting and fun. How many believers and people in general feel this exact way? Feeling trapped where they are and not knowing how to escape and win in life.

I'm Winning All The Time

Chapter 2

Gathering Enough Biblical Knowledge

Then it clicked in my mind that we were doing something wrong.

We did not have enough of the right biblical knowledge, I pondered this and thus declared. So, to win in life, we had to gather enough of the right information from the Word of God to help correct our erroneous thinking. Our error was not totally clear until God spoke to us again through one of the sermons I delivered. It was by God's divine power titled, I'm Winning All the Time..... through Christ. At the time, we were just lying in bed talking about how God's word further declared that we were winning all the time through Christ regardless of what was going on in and around us. We discussed how our finances were upside down, the world's economy was in a state of depression, jobs were scarce, and people were losing their jobs and homes, while businesses were closing down, but we were winning. It was our choice to choose to believe the word of God. We chose to win! It is a choice. Yes, winning is a choice. You too must chose to win in life.

Those words were beginning to click in our minds, not only for me to be inspired to write this dynamic book with my wife's support, of course, but for us to become fully persuaded in realizing that in actuality we are more than conquerors through Christ. Our focus was being redirected towards the truth of God's word; we were no longer alone with only the facts of life. God's word declares in John 8:32 (KJV), "And ye shall know the truth, and the truth shall make you free." This began to say to us the truth saves, delivers and heals. Notice the verse read the truth shall make you free and not the facts! Though that was the toughest temporary season ever for us, we had to reflect on our past victories just as David did on his challenge with Goliath prior to becoming king. The fact was Goliath was bigger and taller than David. The fact was Goliath never lost a physical fight, but the truth was David knew God was on his side; while others doubted as they were afraid and ran away from Goliath. David remembered what God did to him, upon him, with him, for him and through him as he defeated both the lion and the bear.

Therefore, we were winning even in the midst of our most challenging moments, trials and experiences. Furthermore, we had to remember and practice the verses in Romans 5:3 - 5 (KJV) where they read, "3 And not only so, but we glory in tribulations also: knowing that tribulation worketh patience; 4 and patience, experience; and experience, hope: 5 And hope maketh not ashamed; because the love of God is shed abroad in our hearts by the Holy Ghost which is given unto us."

So, in the natural when one thinks of winning, he or she may think of working long hours, hard work or even failing the first few times before winning. However, from a spiritual point of view and being a true born again believer of Jesus Christ, God has declared us to be winners; thereby giving us the ability through the Holy Ghost to do what our normal ability could not do alone. I call this supernatural.

It is supernatural because His super which is the Holy Ghost is added to our natural abilities. For instance, non-biblically speaking, many people get perms in their hair. This perm chemical will cause their hair to look a certain way, but without it their hair would not look that way. Well, it was God's super added to our natural helping us to win in life.

CHAPTER 3

Renewing The Mind

Through our challenges, I discovered some key ingredients to help us win every battle. The first focal point I would like to discuss that will help one to live a winning all the time lifestyle through Christ is **renewing the mind**. Why? Because not only was our mindset not in line with God's thoughts, but we were influenced to think erroneously like so many other born again believers because of the facts of life. First of all, whenever one truly repents from his or her sins and totally turns to God with his or her whole heart, mind and soul, gets saved and filled with His holy ghost, his or her mind does not get saved nor properly renewed automatically. This means one's mind must be renewed daily through hearing God's word on a daily schedule, reading and studying His word regularly, and declaring His word daily. All while setting one's self in the right environment to help create increased thinking towards the Kingdom of God.

The Bible teaches us that the promises of God are not received automatically, but they are received by faith, Galatians 3:13 - 14. It further discusses how lacking knowledge in the things of God could cause one to miss out on the promises of God. Therefore, we must begin to develop a discipline towards learning, understanding and skillfully applying God's word. Becoming kingdom minded required us to retrain our minds. Romans 12:2 (KJV) reads, "And be not conformed to this world: but be ye transformed by the renewing of your mind, that ye may prove what is that good, and acceptable, and perfect, will of God." This verse helped us to properly renew our thought life so that we could receive God's promises for our lives. Again, our thinking was totally offset. This is why we could not receive and experience God's best for our lives at that time, even though we were entitled to God's promises. It's not about the facts alone, but it's about the truth, God's word! Yes, entitled to them, but we did not receive and experience them because of our erroneous thinking.

So, how were we in agreement with God without having the same mind as God? In fact, Amos 3:3 (KJV) asked, "Can two walk together, except they be agreed? Likewise, with Abram whose name was later changed to Abraham, he too needed to renew his mind in order for him to receive God's promises; God's best for his life. In Genesis 12:1 (KJV) God speaks to Abram saying, "Get thee out of thy country, and from thy kindred, and from thy father's house, unto a land that I will show thee." Why did God want Abram to leave his kindred, his family? Was his environment a problem? There could be many thoughts developed from this verse.

However, this was God's way to get Abram's mind conditioned to think totally different from the way he was used to thinking. His environment was erroneously framing his thinking. His environment was more natural minded, with thoughts like show me first and then I will believe. Now God wanted to reframe Abram's thought life so that he could learn, know and develop the mind of God to prepare him for his kingdom assignment. Getting him away from his environment was the best way to get his attention so that he could develop an intimate relationship with God. As a direct result, Abram would become skillfully trained in knowing the voice of God. As it was with many other biblical Christians, each one had to renew his or her thinking in the way God thinks or does things. To further renew one's mind, one must understand that life is choice driven.

Chapter 4

The Law of A Negative Environment

So, we had to learn and obey the law of environment. The law of environment consisted of both a negative and positive environment.

This is the second focal point I would like to share with you, as it helped us in consistently renewing our minds in order to win all the time in life. The word environment means surroundings.

First, I would like to discuss the impacts of a negative environment, as we learned how it could negatively damage you. Your environment could negatively corrupt you as it did to Lot in Genesis chapters 13 – 14:1- end. Lot was surrounded by people who did not believe nor worship his true and living God, which means his environment helped to influence him to think negatively towards God and himself.

Your environment could do several negative things:

1. Your environment could confuse you as it did to the lost son in Luke 15:11 - 16. He found himself in an unknown country sitting there looking at the swine as he was confused as to

who he was. Because of his negative environment, how many Christians today are confused about who they truly are in Christ? They're looking primarily at the facts and are not truly focused on the truth.

2. Your environment could restrict or limit you to its limitations. Let's look at a non-biblical example. Take an apple seed and place it in a small box. After doing your due diligence, such as giving the seed all that it needs to properly grow, when it grows, the apple tree will grow according to its environment. Why did it grow according to its environment? Was it because it is a law? Yes, it is a law. Your environment could be working against you

even when you are not aware of it.

3. Your environment could potentially pull you away from God as it could cause you to doubt God's word even though God has clearly spoken to you about your promises...your blessings...your victories. Yes, it is personal. Your promises! For example, God had clearly spoken to Moses to send twelve spies to Canaan so that they could possess that land as an inheritance unto them. However, when they returned with their reports, ten of the twelve spies had a negative report even though they all were instructed to go and possess the land.

As the ten spies shared their negative reports with the crowd in Numbers 13:28, 31b and 33b (KJV) saying, 28 "Nevertheless the people be strong that dwell in the land, and the cities are walled, and very great: and moreover we saw the children of Anak there. 31b We be not able to go up against the people; for they are stronger than we. 33b and we were in our own sight as grasshoppers, and so we were in their sight."

As you can clearly see, the ten spies' minds were negatively impacted by their own negative thoughts, and by what they had seen and experienced regardless of what God had clearly told Moses to tell them. Their reports signified that their minds were not in agreement with God even though God said they could possess this land. The ten spies did express doubt unto God while King Solomon's negative environment pulled him away from God. His environment changed his heart against God even though God revealed Himself to Solomon. Twice He instructed him beforehand not to surround himself with certain women, whose minds and purposes were not willing and ready to serve his God, The Great I Am, 1 Kings 11: 1 - 13. Why, because their intentions were to change his heart against his God to serve their God, Baalim.

The same thing happened to the children of Israel in the book of Judges Chapter 3:6 - 7. They too were warned beforehand by Moses, while dwelling among the Canaanites, Hittites, Amorites, Perizzites, Hivites and the Jebusites, not to surround themselves with them because their environment did not serve the God of Israel. This caused them to forget about their God and serve the God of Baalim and the groves. As you can see, in order to develop the mind of God to win in life, one's environment plays a major role in his or her mental and spiritual development.

The supporting scriptures that I am about to share with you helped us to realize and recognize the importance of our environment and how it has the potential to corrupt one's thinking, in terms of: Proverbs 13:20b, 1 Corinthians 5:9 - 13, 1 Corinthians 15:33 and 2 Corinthians 6:14 -

16. As they influenced our thinking and changed our mindset, they created a better atmosphere, which was required to produce kingdom thoughts and results. This developed us into being more conscious minded and enabled our perspective towards the Kingdom of God to forever be positively impacted. More so than ever before, we became fully persuaded to pursue having the knowledge and proper understanding of God so that our old thoughts could be permanently replaced with the thoughts of God. Thereby, we received the results of God. There was not a better way for us to develop and retrain our thinking than for us to surround ourselves with the right environment to bring about a spiritual

Change and a physical manifestation in our lives.

I'm Winning All The Time

Chapter 5

The Law of A Positive Environment

Now, I would like to discuss the impacts of a positive environment. In order to develop the right behavior or attitude from the right environment to win all the time in life, we must begin to develop and adapt to separating ourselves from certain friends or people who will corrupt or contaminate our thought life.

For example, 1 Corinthians 15:33 (KJV) reads, "Be not deceived: evil communications corrupt good manners." I looked at this verse this way; because of the law of environment, we could become corrupted while in our own environment. Therefore, we must surround ourselves with people who are headed in the same direction as we are, and with those who have already accomplished what we are pursuing.

I thought, yes it might feel uncomfortable witnessing other's success, in terms of being pushed, challenged and inspired to reach for more. However, without the push, challenge and inspiration, how would we accomplish new and better territory in our thought life and have a better life style? We needed to learn more about how to properly operate this law. In order to get it to work for us in every situation, we began to develop, grow and cultivate positive relationships, because we knew we were on our way to somewhere special!

It is a law. You must feel and know you are on your way to somewhere special and everybody cannot go with you. Again, I thought if the law can work against us, then it can also work for us with enough of the proper knowledge and understanding coupled with the proper application. Say this, "I can get the law of environment to work for me rather than against me." Therefore, we began to surround ourselves with certain people who helped to enhance our Godly expectations for the promises of God through our thought life. Our environment today consists of people who are progressive, willing to take Godly chances, those who will push us forward instead of holding us back, and those who praise and worship God.

It is something supernatural about being in the right atmosphere of God. I call it the atmosphere of faith. The right atmosphere.... That is to say the atmosphere of faith could cause you to do something positive for yourself, even for others that you would have never done for or that you have not done in a very long time. For instance, in Matthew 14:27b - 29 KJV, Peter is on the boat with his fellow disciples seeing Jesus walk on water appearing as a spirit scared and troubled. Jesus says to them, "Be of good cheer; it is I; be not afraid. Peter answered and said, Lord, if it be thou, bid me to come unto thee on the water. And He said, Come." Because Peter was in the right environment or in the atmosphere of faith, it challenged, pushed and inspired him to think outside of the box. It created possibilities for him. It created different views and opportunities for him and those who were around him. His environment challenged him to do something that he had never done before. Yes, he might have been scared, timid, and even doubtful about the fact that in the natural it was impossible to do, yet he tried.... he stepped out in faith... he chose to believe the spoken word of the Lord. He believed when Jesus said, "Come." His environment influenced him with his faith to step out of the boat and walk on water towards Jesus. It was supernatural. Being in the right atmosphere will encourage you to think supernatural thoughts, possible thoughts and creative thoughts. So, to win in life, one must correctly believe that success is possible for him or her even while facing dangerous and unbelievable situations. Others may be scared to believe God's word, but you believe and go for it! Step out in faith.

Did you notice no one else stepped out of the boat besides Peter? Why was that? Could it be possible that others did not believe that it was possible to walk on water even at the command of Jesus? Could it be possible that others did not believe it was possible to do as Jesus did because no one else has done it before? Could you not be the first to graduate, although you knew that no one else had started and completed high school or even college? Peter's mind was being renewed for kingdom commitment. His perspective was being shifted in a miraculous way. Peter had to make a conscious decision to put the Word of God first even though his situation looked hopeless and scary. As with Peter, our new environment will help us to renew our minds for a kingdom commitment. I say

Kingdom commitment because each Christian must make a kingdom commitment decision to put God (His word) first no matter what because what matters most has not changed, which is the Word of God.

This is a determination, no matter what your situation is. You must set a course of action based on the Word of God and go above and beyond with a compelling desire and requirement to please God. So, we began to think in order to be productive as a citizen in the Kingdom of God, we must not only possess our minds, but also manage our will.

Chapter 6

Learning to Manage One's soul

This is another focal point I would like to address concerning learning to manage one's will in order to win in life. One's will is another feature of one's soul. Your soul consists of your mind, will, emotions, imaginations and intellect. To win in the Kingdom of God, your will must be subject to the use of God at all times no matter what your physical senses tell you, shows you or what your current situation may be. This meant we had to learn how to yield our will totally to God in order to change our thought life, attitude, habits and situation.

For example, turn your bible to John Chapter 20: 24 – 25 (KJV). It is there where Jesus teaches about the importance of yielding one's will totally to God to overcome difficulties. In fact, zoom in on verse 25. Here, Thomas has a problem yielding his will to what the other disciples says to him concerning Jesus' resurrection. Mind you, Jesus forewarned them of this situation. Thomas says to them, "Except I shall see in his hands the print of the nails, and put my finger into the print of the nails, and thrust my hand into his side, I will not believe." Notice, he says, "I will not believe." Thomas has trouble believing because he has trouble yielding his will. You must first learn to yield your will to believe. Sometimes this can be difficult due to one's upbringing. Though Jesus met Thomas at his developmental stage in life, he yet had trouble developing a will to yield. So, how can one win over fear, doubt, lack, unbelief and his or her personal challenges if he or she do not learn to yield himself or herself to the will of God, regardless of what one sees, does not see or how one may even feel? This principle can and will work in life for anyone who chooses to yield to believe.

Another feature to win in life is learning how to control one's emotions. We had to learn how to control our emotions during the early process of renewing our minds to gain and maintain victory; while being faced with many different challenges. Our emotions were getting the best of us, as we were focusing on the facts rather than the truth. I say controlling your emotions because when you are in a faith fight, your emotions can get out of control. We were in a faith fight, but we did not know it. A faith fight! How many believers and people in general are in a faith fight and do not know it? To be declared a winner, there must have been some sort of opposition… some form of a challenge, right! I say a faith fight because whenever there is an opposition, a challenge or even a rejection, a fight has started. It has begun and the faith fight is on. Many do not label it or call it a faith fight; it is usually called a turndown, which usually happens due to not knowing that your faith is to be properly used in order to win the fight. You are in a faith fight as we were. During this time, you must learn to control your emotions and minimize your frustration.

As our faith was being challenged in 2008, as it is still being challenged today, thoughts were entering our minds like are we going to lose our home, car, business and so on? Our emotions were trying to control and carry us away from our biblical beliefs and faith into fear, doubt and unbelief. Again, the facts were becoming more and more the truth. It was our actual situation and circumstances appearing as the truth! The facts were stacked against us.

We began to reflect on two passages of scriptures. The first passage can be found in Luke 21:19 (KVJ) where it reads, "In your patience possess ye your souls." This verse told us as born again believers we can possess our own souls, meaning we can develop and control our thought life as we manage our emotions. Our thought life can work against us, or we can develop it to work for us. Our thought life can be a lifestyle of faith, increase and being likeminded with God. As we can clearly see, our thought life has a direct effect on our emotions.

So, as your thought life increases to be in line with the Kingdom of God, you will have better control over your emotions during your faith fight. The second passage we referred to in developing a renewed mindset for winning all the time is found in Luke 22:39 - 43. After reading these verses, I discovered that Jesus was dealing with His emotions, His will and His obedience to His father. In dealing with controlling His emotion's fight, in verse 42, Jesus expresses a never-the-less attitude. So, as your emotions increase while you're being faced with pressure, opposition, troubles and challenges (as with Jesus), you too must develop a never-the-less attitude no matter what in order to win. In helping us to do so, we had to focus primarily on the truth in God's word and not on the facts that we were challenged with because the facts are subject to change for the better.

As a direct result of renewing our minds with a better perspective, the intellect of God, management of our will, and having control of our emotions, which allowed us to imagine ourselves experiencing God's best, we were able to create a new meaning for our situations and ultimately in our lives as did Jesus in Luke 22:39 - 43. This new meaning that I am talking about helped us to redefine our challenging moments back then and is yet working for us today. We came to understand that just because others were challenged and defeated, did not necessarily mean that we too would be defeated when challenged in a faith fight. We can win! You can win, as you are a winner! So, redefine your moments; give a new meaning to your challenging moments. Learn and declare what God has said about you. Search the scriptures daily to discover what God has said about you!

I'm Winning All The Time

Chapter 7

A New Meaning

Another focal point I would like to discuss is a new meaning. During this time, we noticed that other people were losing their cars, homes, businesses, marriages, ministries and experiencing lack. Simply put, struggling while being defeated. Fear was trying to swallow us up as we watched others get swallowed in their challenges. How others were defeated by their situations strongly projected concern. Referring back to the above passages of scriptures helped us to create a new meaning or redefinition of our moments, as we managed our emotions and kept our frustration at minimum. We began to think just because others were experiencing difficult moments with losses, did not necessarily mean that our results must also end in losses because we are winners and winners always win even when it looks differently.

We learned that we can use our challenging moments as a redefining moment of focus and truth. As Jesus uses the principal of a new meaning or redefinement of His moment in time in Luke 22:39 - 43, He views His task differently in terms of His ability to move His focus from His pain, challenge, and difficult moment to pleasure. As he did that in verse forty-two, then in verse forty-three an angel appeared to him from heaven strengthening, encouraging, inspiring, and motivating him to press forward regardless of his difficult emotional moments. This is where the enemy has tried to get us, he tried to get us not to start what God had placed in our hearts. Winning is what God had placed in our hearts. See, he wants to get you to start something then stop because he wants you to focus more on your current pain, challenges, frustrations and obstacles so that you will not realize that God is moving you from your pain to your pleasure. For instance, let's review some supporting scriptures, which are designed by God to help move you from your current pain into your Godly pleasure by assisting you with developing a new meaning no matter what trouble you're facing. Read Job 36:11 - 12, Isaiah 1:19 – 20, and Malachi 3:10 - 11 (If you are not careful, you may begin to think that giving is defined as painful rather than pleasure like the rich young ruler in Luke 18:18-24). You may ask, how do I get back in the race of winning during or after the pain, failures, disappointments, heartache and setbacks. Well, you develop a "nevertheless moment" to focus more on the joy ahead of you, rather than the current pains in, and around you. Hebrews 12:3 tells you and every believer to greatly consider Christ's challenges and how He endured contradictions while you are being challenged in your life; lest you become wearied and faint in your minds. While you are going through tough moments, reflect on what Christ encountered to help you win in life as He did. Use Him as your perfect example as He is. So, in developing this new meaning or this nevertheless attitude through renewing our minds and surrounding ourselves with an inspiring, motivating and influencing atmosphere, we also recognized a need to understand and skillfully apply biblical belief and faith. We needed to know how to scripturally release both so that we could experience God's consistent best even during rough, tough and challenging times. After all, God's word has not changed. God's word does not change because of changes in our situation. Right! So, I discovered in order to believe God's word, we needed the true knowledge that God's word contains everything that we need in this life. I located this in Ephesians 1:3 (KJV) where it reads, "Blessed be the God and Father of our Lord Jesus Christ, who hath blessed us with all spiritual blessings in heavenly places in Christ." As a direct result, I knew that all we needed to regularly win in this life, regardless of how our current situation may look, it was up to me to choose to believe that our blessings do exist. Yes, they do exist! They exist spiritually even when you do not see them. Comprehending this seemed foolish, as we were experiencing tough times, I thought. But then I realized that the spiritual realm is more so real than the earthly realm. I began to think how could I make a clear association of this scripture to produce manifestations in our lives, as well as others? How could I articulate this scripture in our lives so that it could bring clarity in the lives of others? This book is how; God showed me. I began to associate Ephesians 1:3 to another scripture to help me clearly understand as I write this book. For example, in Genesis 1:1 KJV it reads, "In the beginning God created the heaven and the earth." The bible teaches about the law of order. In applying this principle, I noticed God first created the heaven then He created the earth. This taught us that the earth realm was birth from the spiritual realm, which means the things we see in the earth realm came from a place that we do not see, which is the spiritual realm. Therefore, the spiritual realm is more so real than the earthly realm. How, because the spiritual was created first, while the earthly realm was created from the spiritual realm. For instance, non-biblically speaking, my mother was created before me; I came from her womb. This means she came first, as I was created from her. Though you see my picture on the cover of this book, it does not mean that my mother does not exist because you do not see her picture. Likewise, it is with the earthly realm. It was created from the spiritual realm making the spiritual realm very important, although ~~as~~ you cannot see it as you can the earthly realm. This helped us to believe God's word even though we did not naturally see the spiritual realm. It helped us to release our faith for more even in the midst of failing moments. This helped us to create our new meaning in life.

I'm Winning All The Time

Chapter 8

Biblical Belief

Our biblical belief was our starting point into biblical faith. This is another focal point I would like to share in helping you to win in life. I say biblical belief because we had to accept God's word as true even though we did not have any sense realm evidence to show us otherwise. Notice, I did not say there was no evidence.

Rather, I said we did not have any sense realm evidence because all of our senses told us we were doomed, there was no way out, and it would not get better. Sounds familiar? So, we went to the word of God. God led us to open our bible to John 20:24 – 29 to help us better understand His biblical teaching on what biblical belief truly is as we were being transformed. There we found Jesus giving a lesson on biblical belief to Thomas. Thomas had difficulty with his biblical belief. Our thinking was similar to Thomas' thoughts, in terms of needing to see, touch and feel before acceptance. In fact, in verse twenty-four, Thomas replies to the disciples saying, "Except I shall see in his hands the print of the nails, and put my finger into the print of the nails, and thrust my hand into his side, I will not believe." I understand that I previously discussed the importance of one's will. However, one's will is directly connected to one's biblical belief system because Thomas refused to yield his will to believe God's word and accept God's word as true. He was not operating in biblical belief. He was operating according to his natural senses. Therefore, Jesus furthers his lesson to correct Thomas' biblical belief, as He did with us in verse twenty-nine saying, "Thomas, because thou hast seen me, thou hast believed: blessed are they that have not seen, and yet have believed." I said wow! This was what we were really missing. This was exactly what we needed. This lesson taught us to yield our will to God's word regardless of the fact that we did not naturally see our way out. Knowing God's word is our evidence for victory and the truth for winning. This scripture truly taught us what biblical belief is all about. How do I believe? I simply accept God's word as true and as my evidence, although my situations may show something else. As I learned and I write that our will was directly connected to our belief system as to what we were willing to yield our will to believe.

Chapter 9

Biblical Faith

Biblical faith is when there is a corresponding action in connection with your belief. We also discovered that our will is also connected to our biblical faith because when you know the will of God, you can yield your will to believe and have faith because faith works. We learned that faith works in every circumstance.

Our faith was not properly yielding fruit because our will and our belief systems were out of the will of God. From Jesus' biblical belief teachings to Thomas in John 20:24 - 29, we noticed that biblical belief is accepting God's word as true without having any sense realm evidence. Therefore, biblical faith is having a corresponding action in connection with one's biblical belief. For example, non-biblically speaking, if I have believed (accepted) eating enough fruits and vegetables daily to be healthy to my body, then my faith will show forth a corresponding action in connection with my belief, such as I will eat enough fruits and vegetables daily in order to help my body remain healthy. So, we had to ask ourselves, "Are we sure we are operating in biblical faith?" From reading the scriptures, we saw that when used properly, biblical faith truly works. We found ourselves asking God over and over again for the same things as though God was deaf. Did He hear me? For instance, if I were to ask you right now to take me to Burger King at 1:30 pm for lunch and you said yes, why would I continue asking you over and over again as though I did not hear you? Would it be because I truly did not yield my will to accept what you said was true? You might begin to think that I am crazy, right. You might also say, did he not hear me say yes? Well, we had to learn more about this believing and receiving principle. As we began to read, study and clearly understand Matthew 7:7a where it reads, "Ask and it shall be given you," our minds were being correctly renewed in the things of God. We realized that this scripture revealed to us that God promises to answer all of our genuine prayers and that everything we need for spiritual success has been promised to us, therefore leaving us as His children with no excuse for failure. Failure is not an option because we win! Winning is our covenant right, just as it is your covenant right. Our misunderstanding of scripture stemmed from hearing the wrong words, thinking the wrong way and misinterpreting the scriptures, in terms of Luke 18:1 - 8. In Luke chapter 18:5 - 8, a woman is bothering an unjust judge with her consistent asking. God's word never teaches the believer to bother Him. Our thinking was in line with this woman's thoughts, which was if we bother God through much asking, then he will answer us favorably. He will get in a hurry to answer us, we thought. However, He's the King of all kings and the Lord of lords. You may be asking yourself why did I stop asking God over and over again for the same things in prayer. Well, it's simple, so that I could operate in proper biblical faith. You simply change your petition (request) of asking for the same thing over and over again into prayers of thanksgiving and praise. Like Abraham in Romans 4:20 – 21 (KJV), which reads, "He staggered not at the promise of God through unbelief; but was strong in faith, giving glory to God; And being fully persuaded that, what he had promised, he was able also to perform." As we were learning more about biblical faith, we learned our responsibility in receiving our desires through our biblical faith. That is, we learned that God wanted us involved. It's a partnership. Remember, biblical faith is having a corresponding action in connection with yielding one's will to God and what one has believed as true. Therefore, your responsibility in obtaining your desires in prayer is there must be a corresponding action. The bible is clear about God wanting us involved in His plan of action. For instance, from Mark 16:20, I discovered two points that I would like to share with you, in terms of: (1) As Jesus sent forth his disciples and as they preached everywhere, the Lord was working with them. God is always going to work with you as you work the principle of biblical faith and having a corresponding action in connection with your biblical belief. Thus, yielding your will to God's only and perfect will. (2) Not only did I discover that God would work with me, but He would also confirm His word concerning the very thing I desired in prayer. For example, Psalm 37:5 (KJV) reads, "Commit thy way unto the Lord; trust also in him; and he shall bring it to pass." So, when God gives you a plan of action and you put it into proper action, there will be actions corresponding with your dimension of faith. Therefore, if you release your biblical belief for a job, but you never get up and look in the want ads, and never go out seeking employment, then you are not putting your faith into action because faith without works is dead, being alone.

Chapter 10

Release Your Faith

We also discovered the importance of releasing our faith for what we believed God for according to His word. We were speaking more so about our current situation, rather than speaking in agreement with God's word while praying. We had to properly learn how to release our faith according to the word of God. As we were learning this principle, it led us to think and ask each other, "Are we speaking in agreement with what we have prayed for?" See, your thought life is directly connected to the words that you speak?" In fact, the bible teaches that one has to think of a thing before he or she can actually act it out. In other words, your thoughts precede your way of action. Your thoughts and the words you speak are powerful. They can manifest what you do not physically see, whether good or bad. In Mark 11:23 (KJV), for instance, it discusses a powerful principle that caught my attention about what we can have whenever we pray and believe without doubting in our hearts. It reads, "For verily I say unto you, that whosoever shall say unto this mountain, Be thou removed, and be thou cast into the sea; and shall not doubt in his heart, but shall believe that those things which he saith shall come to pass; he shall have whatsoever he saith." So then, the bible is very clear in that I will have what I say, if I choose to believe and not doubt in my heart. The words that I say out of my mouth, believing in my heart and receiving them are the things that I will have and possess in my life. Wow! Also from this verse, one makes the transfer from the spiritual realm (world) into the natural, touchable, tangible realm by the words of one's mouth. Here are more scriptures that support the principle of "Speaking in agreement with what you've prayed for," please read them at your leisure. Proverbs 18:21, Matthew 12:37, Romans 10:10, and Hebrews 13:15. These scriptures helped us to understand the importance of the use of our words, they also helped us to create a biblical faith confession. Now, you may be saying to yourself or aloud what is a biblical faith confession? Since words are used to release one's faith, implementing a faith confession is vitally important, like in Mark 11:23. I can have whatsoever I say out of my mouth when I believe and not doubt in my heart according to the word and will of God. I could also manifest what I do not currently see, like in Genesis 1:3, 4, 6, 9, 11, 14, 20, 24, 26, 28, 29, and 31 where God spoke, and He saw everything that came out of His mouth come into existence. In other words, He said what He wanted to see, not what He saw because He already knew what his situation was. Speaking God's words from your mouth as you believe in your heart and not doubt is how to release your biblical faith into the atmosphere. So, you release your faith by the words of your mouth, as God did. He used His words to create just what He wanted to see in the earth realm. This is clearly done by way of you depositing God's word richly into your heart through the hearing of His word and speaking His word daily. Are you using your words to speak into existence just what you want to see, even though what you currently see might not appear promising? Are you afraid to speak what you want to see because you fear the danger of it not coming to pass? Wow! I heard many believers say, "I am not saying what God's word says about my situation because what if it does not happen." Well, we were speaking more so of what we see with our natural eyes, rather than what we want to see with our natural eyes. We had to learn to see the unseen through our spiritual eyes. What a powerful principle to use. The power is truly in your mouth while you believe. Therefore, to explain what a faith confession is, let's go to Romans 10:10 (KJV) where it reads, "For with the heart man believeth unto righteousness; and with the mouth confession is made unto salvation." That word confession does not necessarily mean one confesses his or her sins to man, but rather it means to speak in agreement with or to say the same as. In essence, I learned the bible is speaking out loud to its readers and hearers that it is with the heart (the inward man) that one believes, and with the mouth confession is made in agreement with what God says about us and our situations! So, a faith confession is a statement that one chooses to declare from the word of God in agreement with God's word regardless of how one feels, regardless of what one naturally sees, and regardless of what one's circumstances are. No matter how things looked, my wife and I chose to no longer tolerate doubting and being in fear of a negative outcome. We chose to take God at His word. Why, because what mattered most had not changed, which was the Word of God, even though our situations had. For example, In Genesis 1:2, it discusses how there was voidness all around and the earth was without form and darkness was upon the face of the deep, yet God began to change things by what He believed and said! Again, He did not speak what He saw, and He did not speak what the circumstances were. Why? Because He knew what the circumstances were, just like you should know what your circumstances are. So, to see and experience better things in life start declaring what you want to see in your life. Start believing things can get better for you. Start believing that things have gotten better for you even when you do not physically see it. Speak it! Declare it from your mouth. God said what He desired to see on the earth in Genesis 1:3 (KJV), "And God said, Let there be light: and there was light." After reading this scripture, I immediately thought this is an example of the God Kind Of Faith that calls things that are not as though they were. What's not in your life? Now, start calling into your life what's not there. With this God Kind of Faith coupled with our beliefs, like Jesus, we were able to say, "Let there be..." to our situation and by faith call into existence our need(s) and desire(s) according to God's will.

For example, you can begin to confess the

following scriptures as we did, and learn to confess them daily for your development in winning throughout the day and during your daily prayer time:

1. Psalm 103:1 – 5 (KJV) "Bless the Lord O my soul: and all that is within me, bless his holy name. 2 Bless the Lord, O my soul, and forget not all his benefits: 3 Who forgiveth all thine iniquities; who healeth all thy diseases; 4 Who redeemeth thy life from destruction; who crowneth thee with lovingkindness and tender mercies; 5 Who satisfieth thy mouth with good things; so that thy youth is renewed like the eagle's."

2. Isaiah 53:4 - 5 (KJV) "Surely he hath borne our griefs, and carried our sorrows: yet we did esteem him stricken, smitten of God, and afflicted. 5 But he was wounded for our transgressions, he was bruised for our iniquities: the chastisement of our peace was upon him; and with his stripes we are healed."

3. Romans 4:17 (KJV) "(As it is written, I have made thee a father of many nations,) before him whom he believed, even God who quickeneth the dead, and calleth those things which be not as though they were."

As a true born again believer filled with the precious gift of the Holy Spirit, I began to use these scriptures to help us win in life, even though it seemed as though we were losing in the natural realm. I realized we had the power to use our faith confession to our advantage in spite of what we were facing. I would like to encourage you today to begin using your mouth to help release and increase your faith with demonstration. Just like the above examples, you have the power within you to create what is not there in the physical realm. For instance, non-biblically speaking, while growing up as a kid, just before it got dark outside, my mother would call my name, my brother and sister's names to come in the house. Though we were not there with her at the time, when we heard her voice from a distance, we began to make ourselves go home. We appeared. She called that which was not physically there to appear. Yes, it might have taken some time, but we showed up on time. Likewise, if you have a little dog that ran away from you while being walked, when you are ready for the dog to come to you, what would you do? You call the dog's name, right? When you call the dog's name, the dog later appears. Well, the faith confession system works the same way. So, to win in life all the time, you have to begin to discipline yourself as we did and are yet doing to this determining course of action, no matter what. Remember, what matters most has not changed. God created and used the above principles as demonstrations for every believer to win all the time, no matter what season you may find yourself. As we had to discover that God created us as winners, we want you to know that you too are a winner! You are a conqueror! You are a champion. You are victorious. As a true born again believer, victorious living belongs to you. Victorious living is yours. You are to win all the time. Say this, "I am a winner no matter what is going on around and in me. I win all the time in every situation!" Today, I win! I will every day. Tomorrow, I win! Today, my wife and I have been winning our battles through our attitude, biblical belief and faith, environment, managing both our will and emotions and our faith confessions. We win! You Win!

Chapter 11

Patience

There is a bonus point I would like to share with you. You must know, understand and skillfully apply the patience principal. This biblical principal has tremendously helped us in understanding the process to overcome our struggles and faith fights. This principal is also a vital tool to learn, understand and skillfully apply to help you alleviate your frustrations as it did for us, while using both your biblical believing and biblical faith principals. Many believers become overwhelmingly frustrated in life due to not properly understanding the time factor principal involved, while properly exercising their believing and faith principals. For instance, in the book Mark 4:26 - 28 (KJV) it reads, "And he said, So is the kingdom of God, as if a man should cast seed into the ground; 27 And should sleep, and rise night and day, and the seed should spring and grow up, he knoweth not how. 28 For the earth bringeth forth fruit of herself; first the blade, then the ear, after that the full corn in the ear." From these verses, I noticed a process in order to see a manifestation in life. While in Hebrews 10:36

(KJV), it reads, "For ye have need of patience, that, after ye have done the will of God, ye might receive the promise." These scriptures are saying to the born again believer or a person, as you speak daily God's word and act on God's word, you might not always see an immediate manifestation of what God has led you to say or do. However, notice I did not say you will not see or experience a manifestation. So many believers and people lose their faith, hope and sense of focus due to not clearly understanding the time factor that's involved in applying the patience principal. Every great success takes time. Every great story takes time to develop. Growth takes time. Change takes time. Proper development takes time. It took time for God to create heaven and earth. For instance, Genesis 2:2 states "And on the seventh day God ended His work which He had made; and He rested on the seventh day from all His work which He had made. As a direct result, many think, say and believe but because they have not seen the promised manifestation within a certain time frame, they figure God must have let them down. Many begin to believe and say "God lied, God is a liar, there is no God." Therefore, you are in need of patience. So, I would like to encourage you with this do not get weary in well doing for you shall reap in due season if you do not faint, Galatians 6:9 (KJV). Remember, slow progress is still progress. Slow increase is still increase. As you progress in winning your battles, it is sure victory…… that you are winning all the time!

I'm Winning All The Time

About the Author

Pastor Donald Robinson is a native of South Florida. He is an educator having obtained an Associate's Degree in Pre-law and a Bachelor's Degree in Political Science. It is his desire to further his education to obtain his Jurist Doctorate Degree. He is the Founder and Pastor of Vision for Christ Ministries International.

Pastor Donald Robinson was called to the office of Pastor/Teacher in February, 2005. Since that time, he has continued to affect the lives of many through his anointed illustrated teaching, preaching and gifted leadership skills. Because of his obedience and dedication to the Lord, many have joined him in this ministry.

Pastor Donald Robinson is dedicated to the sensitivity of the Holy Spirit as it leads him to impact the lives of others. He is truly a Pastor after God's own heart! Both He and his Wife Co-Pastor Lucy are also, proud owners of Josiah's Christian Academy #1 and #2 which are located in the cities of North Lauderdale and Plantation where they serve together as business partners.

Pastor Donald Robinson truly demonstrates exemplary leadership and excellence in this region of the United States. He is an enthusiastic, vibrant, cheerful speaker and a student of God's word. He is one who not only knows God's word, but lives God's word!

Pastor Donald Robinson is a family man. He supports and promotes healthy family relationships which have contributed to the many successful years in his own marriage. He and his wife have been happily married for over 19 years. They have 5 beautiful children along with eight beautiful grandchildren. Pastor Robinson and his lovely wife not only demonstrate characteristics of a successful marriage, but they are passionate teachers of <u>Assembly Required Marriage Seminar</u> taught at various locations throughout South Florida. He and His wife believe marriage is like an unassembled purchased package where **ASSEMBLY IS REQUIRED!**

Vision For Christ Ministries Int.
1950 N.W. 8th Street Pompano Bch, FL 33069
Tel: 786-565-5038
Email: visionforchristministry@gmail.com
www.visionforchristministries.org

www.ingramcontent.com/pod-product-compliance
Lightning Source LLC
Chambersburg PA
CBHW071524080526
44588CB00011B/1547